"The.. .. .. this time developing a man who will become as the Christ of this age. He is above the age of reason and can vote and make decisions for himself, but it is not yet time for him to start his ministry."

"The usefulness of a medium depends upon his or her talent and intelligence, not the depth or style with which he or she works. The other significant factor affecting the quality of a communication is the integrity of both the medium and the spirit using the channel."

"The high end of the scale of psychic or medium-istic ability is reached by tapping into the roots of mysticism. This involves establishing a rapport with the order of the universe—both by understanding it and by participating with it."

"Spooks are not demi-gods. The proper way to relate to them is to realize that the essence of the relationship is *friendship*. Not worship or lordship."

"It's sad more 'Christians' don't appreciate the historical tradition of healing in their own religion. And it's a shame that ministers and priests don't recognize that healing is a *duty* of their office."

—Arthur Ford

FROM HEAVEN TO EARTH:

ARTHUR FORD RETURNS

———————

BY ROBERT R. LEICHTMAN, M.D.

———————

The Eighth In A Series

ARIEL PRESS
THE PUBLISHING HOUSE OF LIGHT
COLUMBUS, OHIO

Second Printing

This book is made possible by gifts
to the Publications Fund of Light.

ARTHUR FORD RETURNS
Copyright © 1979 by Light

ISBN 0-89804-058-2

A BRIEF INTRODUCTION

*for the benefit of readers who are becoming
acquainted with our series*, From Heaven to Earth,
for the first time

Arthur Ford Returns is the eighth in a landmark series of books written by Dr. Robert R. Leichtman. Each book in this series is the transcript of a conversation between Dr. Leichtman and the spirit of a well-known genius or psychic, conducted through the mediumship of David Kendrick Johnson. The interviews, which were mostly conducted in 1973, grew out of an idea of Dr. Leichtman's to write a collection of biographical sketches which would rekindle public interest in the exploration and investigation of the human mind and psychic potential.

As Dr. Leichtman began composing a list of the people he might wish to write about—people such as Ford, William Shakespeare, Edgar Cayce, C.W. Leadbeater, Nikola Tesla, Thomas Jefferson, and Eileen Garrett—it occurred to him that all of them had left the physical plane. Not only that, but they were also all people with whom he had communicated through direct clairaudience at one time or another.

So, rather than just write biographical sketches of them, he reasoned, why not speak to them *directly*—through a medium—and let them talk about their lives, experiences, inspirations, and current thoughts *in their own words!*

The choice of a medium was an easy one. Dr. Leichtman immediately thought of his good friend, David Kendrick Johnson. Dr. Leichtman knew that Mr. Johnson had been ''entertaining'' Cayce, Jung, Madame Blavatsky, and many of the others on his list for quite some time already. And he respected David's talent as a medium to work compatibly with creative and innovative spirits. A first-rate artist in his own right, David has the understanding and competence which make it possible for other creative geniuses to speak through him, mediumistically. So Dr. Leichtman broached the idea. Mr. Johnson responded enthusiastically.

By the time they began the series of interviews, Dr. Leichtman and Mr. Johnson had drawn up a rather impressive list of people to converse with—heavily weighted toward those who had been gifted with unusual inspiration and vision while alive in the physical body. They decided, for example, to contact such outstanding mediums and pioneers in the exploration of life after death as Ford, Cayce, Garrett, and Stewart Edward White. Also making the list were a number of mysterious, ''occult'' personages: Cheiro, the actor-turned-palmist who gained much fame in Europe with his amazing predictions around the turn of the century; the controversial Madame Blavatsky, who helped found the Theosophical Society and who claimed to be in contact with superhuman ''Masters''; and Bishop

Leadbeater, the clergyman who became a clairvoyant and author of many books on the invisible dimensions of life. Rounding out the list were a number of geniuses who obviously had led inspired lives while being less overtly psychic: William Shakespeare; the psychologists Carl Jung and Sigmund Freud; Thomas Jefferson; Nikola Tesla, the electrical genius; and Sir Oliver Lodge, the British physicist, educator, and early psychic investigator.

As the series' title, *From Heaven to Earth*, suggests, the purpose of this project is to acquaint readers with the current thinking of these outstanding individuals, even though they have left their physical bodies and now work on the inner dimensions of reality. Many new ideas about psychology, psychic phenomena, science, literature, human civilization, and the future of mankind are set forth in these conversations—as well as plenty of good humor.

It is not the intent of this series to document the existence of life after death—or the effectiveness of mediumship in contacting the spirits of those who have left their physical bodies. Nor is it necessary, for these matters have been scientifically proven many times over in other writings—indeed, in many of the books written by the people interviewed in this series. The doubting reader will find ample proofs in the works of Sir Oliver Lodge, Stewart Edward White, Eileen Garrett, Madame Blavatsky, C.W. Leadbeater, Arthur Ford—and countless others.

Instead, the interviews in *From Heaven to Earth* are offered as a way of demonstrating that we need not be content with just an echo of great geniuses who have lived and died; their voices can literally be heard again.

Their spirits and ideas can actually return to earth. Heaven is not some faraway place inaccessible to mortals. It can easily be contacted by competent psychics and mediums who have correctly trained themselves—as have Dr. Leichtman and Mr. Johnson. And such contact can produce insights and new ideas of great importance.

A more complete introduction to this series is contained in the first book, Edgar Cayce Returns. *In it, the nature of the mediumistic trance, the origins of this specific project, and the value of creative genius are discussed in detail. For information on ordering this first volume in the series, please see page 87 in this volume.*

—Carl Japikse
ARIEL PRESS

ARTHUR FORD RETURNS

For half a century, Arthur Ford was possibly the world's best known link between heaven and earth. He began his career in the early 1920's as an ordained minister in Kentucky, but soon became much more than that. For Arthur Ford was also an unusually gifted medium and clairvoyant. At first, he hoped to blend his psychic talents with his ministry, but found the churches he so much wanted to serve unreceptive. So, he began focussing his efforts more on using his mediumistic skills in the occult work of helping others—and in this way found those who needed his assistance. During his lifetime, Ford brought comfort and reassurance to tens of thousands of people, by relaying messages to them from deceased relatives. Through lectures, he helped many more peek behind the veils of consciousness that separate this life from the inner worlds. For some, he set an example that was their first exposure to the real workings of the spiritual life. And, near the end of his career, he was also able to inspire a number of open-minded clergy-men and lay people to work at reviving the mystical and psychic experience in Christianity.

Yet the real value of his work and talents is often obscured by the complexity of his character and the sensational aspects of his career. And create a sensation he often did.

In the late 1920's, his reputation as a medium already well-established, Ford stunned the world by successfully transmitting a coded message from the spirit of the magician Harry Houdini to his widow. Houdini had always been fascinated with spiritualism and mediums, but from the standpoint of debunking them as frauds. Before he died, however, he promised his wife that if there were an afterlife, he would find a way to communicate a secret message to her. After his death, hundreds of mediums tried to bring through this unknown message, but did not succeed. Ford, how-ever, did—in carefully documented sessions. Hou-dini's widow verified the accuracy of the message. The instant result of this achievement was banner headlines in newspapers throughout the country.

Forty years later, Ford once again gained the head-lines with a spectacular television seance in which the Episcopal Bishop James Pike spoke with the spirit of his son, who had committed suicide. In the session, Bishop Pike became convinced that he was, in fact, communicating with his son—as well as several other friends who had left the physical plane.

Both of these events, however, and a number of others, exposed Ford to a barrage of attack. His suc-cess in contacting Houdini was quickly denounced in the tabloids as fraud, in spite of the testimony of the magician's widow. The Pike seance was similarly condemned. It is suggested that Ford prepared himself before these sittings—and others—by reading newspaper clippings. And yet, the scope and accuracy of the comments made far transcend what had been printed in public records.

In some ways, Ford is an easy figure to attack. What he did was so spectacular that there are many people who are all too willing to believe that it simply could not be done—and therefore must have been done fraudulently. Thus, they interpret every aspect of his life as a sign of cheating. There *is* circumstantial evidence that suggests that Arthur may have cheated occasionally. But the evidence is *only* circumstantial— it is not proof. And it is not hard to build an impressive case attacking the integrity of a person who has died.

There was also a dark side to his character—at one time he was addicted to drugs, and later became an alcoholic. He had trouble with personal relationships, and could be quite sarcastic. Yet he candidly admitted these problems and made no claim to being a saint.

There is danger in getting too caught up in these aspects of Ford's life. To fully understand the value of this man and his work, it is necessary to go beyond the flash of the headlines, the suspicions of fraud, and the flaws of his character. We must view him not just as a psychic and medium, but as a pioneer in new human frontiers—and as a reformer within the old traditions of the church.

Arthur Ford dedicated his life to demonstrating the connection between psychic phenomena and religion. Like many gifted people, he was years ahead of his time. The world, and especially the world of traditional religion, was not ready to acknowledge this connection. Nor was it ready to properly accept his gifts of clairvoyance and mediumship. As a result, he was forced to forge his own way in life, promoting his vision as best he could. He did not always have reliable support for his efforts. He was often considered an outsider—not quite accepted, not quite rejected. Most commonly, his real purpose was overlooked, as people argued about side issues that hardly mattered.

What was his real purpose? Quite simply, it was to demonstrate that there is more to life than meets the eye—that the unknown is knowable to those who refuse to accept pat answers and popular traditions. He held that the Truth will somehow reveal itself to those who cherish it and work vigorously to seek its hidden place.

There are many people in the world who, like Ford, pursue an important vision with courage. In many ways, the difficulties and triumphs of Arthur Ford's life can serve as inspiration to all such pioneers and reformers. What is needed for the advancement of civilization is more *admiration* of the strength of character such people demonstrate—not *condemnation* of their human flaws.

It is valuable to realize that Arthur Ford's life involved great difficulty. At the time he began his psychic work, mediumship was not considered a respectable profession. As a group, mediums and psychics were rejected by most of society, and certainly by the church. How then, was he to go about his mission of rekindling religious interest in the invisible worlds?

He did it by pursuing the higher applications of

mediumship—by advocating those uses of this curious connection between heaven and earth that ennoble the human spirit, enrich the physical life, and inspire people to greater achievement. To be sure, much of his work involved the ordinary expressions of psychic and mediumistic talent—giving proof of the survival of the dead and using clairvoyance to advise physical people experiencing difficulties. But he also did much to promote the mystical and religious aspects of these phenomena. He did this not to cloak his professional activities with an aura of respectability—the motive of so many psychics and mediums—but because he was dedicated to an important ideal of life.

In his lectures, Ford often dwelt on the fact that the origins of Christianity—and other major religions as well—are steeped in profound mystical happenings, psychic revelations, and miraculous healings. A careful examination of the history of Christianity confirms this fact. In the first few centuries of its existence, the church was composed principally of informal groups in which psychic, mystic, and mediumistic phenomena were commonly pursued, and in which spiritual healing was accepted as natural. To the early Christians, all these pursuits were a normal part of religious worship, probably because they reflected the example of Jesus and the apostles.

With this inspiration to guide him, Ford set out to encourage the church to give birth once again to the very virtues that marked its beginnings. If Christianity espouses belief in a life after death, why not prove that this survival is a fact? Ford did. If ministers and priests claim that the love of God redeems and heals, why not incorporate spiritual healing into the church's service? Ford did. If the church steadfastly proclaims the reality and immanence of invisible, divine forces, then why not show people how those divine forces operate? Ford did. At times, he found receptive audiences. At other times, people were more intrigued by the sensational aspects of his work—or more preoccupied with proving him either evil or deceitful.

Practical Christianity is meant to be a solacing power that supports us in our daily needs. Through his own personal difficulties and struggles, Ford discovered how meaningful that solacing power can be. In turn, he sought to share this awareness with others, so that they might be supported and helped, too.

Certainly the thousands of hours Ford spent relaying messages from the spirits of deceased humans to relatives still in the physical plane, reassuring them of their continued existence, was an example of the solace of practical Christianity. The time of death is often one of great sorrow and grief. The ability to show a portion of heaven to those still on earth must therefore be deeply religious in nature. Moreover, dedicating one's talent to such work is surely an act of compassion for those who suffer. The smugly pious who condemn mediumship on tenuous theological tenets would do well to look into their hearts and examine what it means to act with Christian love and faith. If they cannot find it there, they can find an example in the work of Arthur Ford.

The practical uses of mediumship in Christianity do not stop with comforting the bereaved, however. Of far greater significance, to Ford at least, were the possibilities open to clergymen who develop psychic and mediumistic talents of their own. A clairvoyant minister would actually be able to see angelic presences and describe them to his congregation. A mediumistic priest or pastor might be able to invoke the inspiration of saints or apostles, to guide him in his sermon, his counseling, or his personal understanding. Or, such a clergyman, by providing an exceptionally clear connection between heaven and earth, might be able to focus far more love and healing power to his congregation than the ordinary minister possessed by faith alone.

The possibility of such uses of mediumship and psychic ability, Ford found, was shocking to many "Christians." That, in turn, was shocking to Arthur, and should be shocking to any intelligent person. Why should Christians, who profess to believe in the divine agency of love and wisdom, reject actual demonstrations of divine love and wisdom?

Ford tried to reform each of the worlds he cared so much about—the mainstream Christian church and the "outcast" world of mediums and psychics. He knew that the higher aspects of the religious experience—the mystical revelations of God's love—could only be reached through the use of the higher forms of psychic awareness. So he carried that message to the churches. And he likewise knew that the usual application of psychism and mediumship for fortune telling and parlor games were child's play compared to the more spiritual applications. So he took that message to his friends and colleagues in the psychic world.

Psychic awareness and mystical awareness are two branches of the same tree. Although some people are all too ready to reject psychic phenomena as irrelevant or dangerous to the spiritual life—and Ford encountered plenty who believed this—he knew that the same eyes which can study the dirt on the ground can be lifted up to view the heavens. *Man's ability to see, whether physically or clairvoyantly, is not inherently dangerous or evil, and it is folly to think that it is.* The medium or psychic who pursues petty phenomena is no more evil than the self-righteous bigot who condemns him with threats of hellfire and brimstone. Both are directing their vision toward the lower, unspiritual elements of life. Ford hoped to inspire both to see the truly mystical dimensions of life.

He also sought to promote spiritual healing as a valid part of Christian stewardship. Through his clairvoyance, Ford was able to perceive directly the value of prayer in facilitating healing. Yet few churches in his day—or even now—paid anything more than lip service to this foundation block of Christianity. So, like a good gadfly, he tried to stir up interest and activity in spiritual healing. He preached the simple and sane message that divine forces are to be *used*, not just worshipped. The rising interest in spiritual healing in this country today is in large measure a result of the often overlooked or undervalued work of Arthur Ford.

Near the end of his career, Ford helped start an organization of ministers and lay people, the Spiritual Frontiers Fellowship, for the purpose of promoting these ideals of mediumship, mystical awareness, and healing. It was anticipated that this group would be able to continue carrying these ideals into the mainstream of the Christian church. While this has not yet worked out as well as hoped, Ford's basic ideals are still well worth pursuing. Some traditions, especially in religion, become enshrined in their own weight and momentum, changing very slowly. The fact that Ford, and others like him, have been able to bring some new life into the modern religious experience is a tribute far more substantial than all the sensational headlines of a long career.

To me, Arthur Ford set an example of courage and dedication. His life is as remarkable for its achievements as it is for its tragedies and struggles. In the interview that follows, I did discuss with him his personal difficulties, and questioned him about the persistent reports about cheating. I felt he should have the chance to clear the air. But I was far more interested— and hope most readers will be, too—in the noble and mystical side of Arthur Ford.

The Arthur Ford I talked to is far removed from the image of Ford many people have created in their minds. I did not talk to Arthur Ford the alcoholic, nor did I speak to Arthur Ford the exhausted and irritable individual he sometimes became. I did not speak to anyone who was impatient or sarcastic or depressed. Instead, I talked to the spiritual essence that not so long ago expressed itself through the physical Arthur Ford.

Spirits do change after they pass over to ''the other side.'' So did Mr. Ford. He has risen above some of the limitations of his personality and is more in touch with the ideals that motivated him during life. Occasionally, those ideals were not fully expressed, and perhaps even tarnished, during his physical life. But the wonderful nature of ideals is that they never lose their potency or value when inadequately expressed— just their charm and appeal.

One of the subjects that comes up in the interview that follows is a question about two readings Ford did for the Korean evangelist Sun Myung Moon, at Mr. Moon's request. At the time these readings were held in the early 1960's, Mr. Moon's Unification Church was largely unknown. Since then, in part on the strength of quoted statements purportedly made by Ford—statements that Ford said were quoted out of context—Moon and his church have grown in influence and controversy. Essentially, Moon claimed that Ford hailed him as a new Messiah. Ford denied any such endorsement. I thought it would be valuable to ask the spirit of Arthur Ford for further clarification of this episode. What he says about it is startling and of interest to any spiritually-minded person.

I was also delighted that Ford shared some of his interview time with his friend in spirit, Fletcher. As fans of Ford's work will know, Fletcher was Arthur's principal ''spirit guide'' during the long course of his career. It was Fletcher who gave most of the messages through the entranced Ford, relaying comments from discarnate spirits to relatives in the audience, answering philosophical questions, and directing each seance. Fletcher appears briefly at the beginning of the interview, and then comes back for a longer visit later on.

In the interview, Fletcher and Arthur speak through the mediumship of my good friend, David Kendrick Johnson. I ask most of the questions, but am joined in the questioning at one point by a friend we shall call Harry White. The first spirit to appear is Rosie, who is David's spirit guide or control. Rosie is a very feminine lady with an impish sense of humor. Yet she is also a powerful person who tolerates no nonsense, in spite of her girlish wit. Ordinarily, she ''warms up'' the medium prior to the appearance of the spirits to be interviewed. She also serves as a "mistress of cere-monies" for the proceedings. Since much of the inter-view to follow deals with mediumship, I thought it appropriate to ask Rosie to talk a little about her role with David first.

Rosie: The house is officially haunted. [*Giggling.*]
Leichtman: It is now, yes. Before you leave, Rosie, would you care to state for the record just who you are and what you do for David at the beginning of each of these sessions?
Rosie: I am David's great-great-great grand-mother. He and I have a more important inner planes relationship that extends back several thousand years, but I will leave that unidentified, if you please. We are very close in the inner planes as spirits.

David's very comfortable with me as a spirit guide because we know each other so well. David and I have somewhat similar temperaments, although he is a gentleman at the moment. I know many people think it's funny that I come in so girlish and giggly. I enjoyed being a girl, and I don't see why I should have to give that up. Besides, David likes a good laugh and a good joke.

While I'm talking to you now, he is not quite into his trance state. But it's easier for him if I hold forth while he's getting out of his body. That gives him a chance to get comfortable on the inner planes before a strange spirit comes in. If the new spirit came in too fast, it would be a bit of a jolt.

The subconscious mechanism through which medi-umship works is very complex. Part of my work as a spirit control involves activating and adjusting David's

ROSIE

system so it will function smoothly. You know, the phenomenon of mediumship takes a lot more than just the ability to fall asleep. [*Laughter.*] There's a great deal of technical knowledge and skill that must be contributed by the spirit control.

I don't run a school for spirit guides, but I've been spooking for several thousand years. And if I do say so myself, I'm pretty good. Many times people have spirit guides that are new at the job, and I can kind of show them the ropes.

Fletcher is objecting very strongly. He says he doesn't really sound quite like me.

Leichtman: Yes, I know.

[*A pause ensued, while Rosie withdrew from David's body, and Fletcher entered.*]

Fletcher: This is Fletcher.

Leichtman: Greetings.

Fletcher: We're still shoving David out, if you will. He feels the same way toward me that he feels toward Rosie. It's not a feeling in the physical sense. It's a feeling like—well, it's akin to friendship, I guess. Anyway, he trusts us to guard the body while he's out, so he doesn't worry too much. That's another important function we perform.

Leichtman: Yes, I can understand.

Fletcher: Once the medium's subconscious is warmed up, the spirit control's main function is to act as a master or mistress of ceremonies, and to gather material on the inner planes. In this project, Cecil George [the individual who coordinated the project from the inner planes] is doing the bulk of this. But we're orchestrating the actual appearances of the spirits. David also helps a lot—just as Arthur often would help me after he got comfortable on the inner planes.

Leichtman: I suppose you also coordinate the messages between the discarnates and the physical people.

Fletcher: Oh, yes. With you, for example, Martha sees to it that the right spook is around to give you an idea when you need it. Martha is an expert at cramming an idea through your head. In a way, Rosie is an expert in cramming something through David's head. I'm being a bit facetious, but that is essentially what happens. Someone like Rosie or I, when I was working with Arthur, can interact with a medium in this way. It is something like being the head telephone switchboard operator, although that's not an exact analogy.

Leichtman: I'm very eager to ask a question which may be out of context now, but I'll ask it anyway. Perhaps Arthur will comment on it, too. Why is it that so many spirit guides seem to be American Indians?

Fletcher: Oh, Bob, you know the answer to that, and I know you know. But I'll give it to you for the record. The names that spooks frequently give when they're "coming through" aren't the names they ever had in life. Many times they will give you not a name but a reference. It's like a dial code on a telephone. Some of these codes come out sounding like an English version of an Indian name: Running Deer, Red Feather, this sort of thing. They aren't actually Indian names, though. They are just the "telephone numbers" of the spooks.

Many spirits don't use the names that they had in life because they are aware that the physical people at the sitting are very much in awe of famous names. The spooks would prefer that their messages not be blocked out by the glamour of their fame, but listened to. Also, many beings on the other side are very modest, and they would prefer not to be known by a ''living'' name.

Now, as it happens, Rosie was in fact an Indian lady. But her real name was Anna. She also had an Indian name which would have to be said something like ''Latona Cecilia,'' only that is not exactly correct. It can be roughly translated as ''Little Wild Rose.'' This was a nickname she liked at one time in life, so she uses it as a spirit guide.

Leichtman: So there actually *are* a few American Indian spirit guides?

Fletcher: There are a few American Indians. There are a few East Indians, too. But just because one has incarnated a few times as an American Indian doesn't mean that person is essentially an American Indian soul.

Leichtman: Okay.

Fletcher: You were an East Indian one time, and there would be a great deal of laughter in the room if I told you what the English translation of your East Indian name was.

Leichtman: Forget it. [*Laughter.*]

Fletcher: In India it was considered a rather graceful name, but it doesn't render itself into English in that way.

Leichtman: I suppose it means ''glittering toe-nails,'' or something like that. Don't answer. [*More laughter.*]

Fletcher: More like ''glittering cobra skin.'' [*Tittering.*] We're about ready for Arthur. I reserve the right to come back.

[*There followed a pause, while Fletcher switched with Arthur Ford.*]

Arthur Ford: Before you ask questions, Doctor, I would like to set the tenor of the afternoon, if I may. I notice my name is in the papers once again. I'm being accused of fraud—because certain clippings and things were found in my files. I would like to make a statement about this.

It is obvious that an intelligent medium, when called upon to do a reading, would do a bit of advanced research on the matter. This is not cheating— it's priming the pump. As has already been indicated in these conversations, working through a medium is a little like playing the piano and having it come out as conversation and body language. It's a bit like working a marionette, in a way. The people who come through this mouth and body are somewhat limited by this personality's language patterns and physical movements and basic intelligence. So, it only makes good sense to do a bit of research before a medium does a sitting. It doesn't mean he's cheating; it doesn't mean he's going to be spouting a lot of information that he's read somewhere. It doesn't work that way. It means that the medium has put in "keys" for the spirit to play on a bit better. Does that make sense to you?

Leichtman: Oh, yes.

Ford: For instance, David is desperately trying to wade through a pamphlet you gave him about one of the gentlemen you're planning to interview for this project [Nikola Tesla]. He doesn't understand very much of it, and so it seems he's not going to be doing all of the channeling for that particular interview.

I'll tell you something funny: David was very nervous when it came to sitting for Leadbeater, because he had only read maybe two paragraphs of his books. He had read some of *There Is A River* but not much of anything else about Edgar Cayce. The writings of Madame Blavatsky give him headaches, so he puts them down very quickly. The sessions when they came through went all right, but why shouldn't he be encouraged to prepare himself? After all, we spirits prepare *ourselves*—these seances aren't spontaneous, you know. [*Ironically*] David *has* read some of my writings, but maybe I can get something straight through his mouth—in spite of that! [*Laughter.*]

With the Tesla sitting, however, it is only natural that both of you are doing what research you can. You are better equipped to understand some of Tesla's ideas than David is. After all, David is an artist and not especially turned on by mechanics or physics or anything of that sort. He could read a book on the gentleman and understand about a third of it, and you could understand maybe two-thirds of it. [*Humorously*] When you do the sitting, maybe between the two of you, you will get something right.

Okay, I'll let you ask questions, since you're about ready to burst.

Leichtman: No, I'm not really bursting, but there are some questions I did want to ask. How often do you think the average medium or psychic is tempted to fudge readings? Is this a common problem?

Ford: I can talk from my own experience. When I got to be well-known, there were a great number of demands put on my time. Whenever that happens, there can be real temptations to fudge or cheat, just to make things go a little easier. I wish I could have.

Leichtman: Could have what?

Ford: Cheated—but I didn't. The pressure on a psychic or medium to produce readings can be very uncomfortable. You start resenting the whole business, which isn't right. And you start feeling that you have no time for yourself. It seems like it would be so easy just to say anything. I often thought it would be a lot easier to say something other than what I was getting psychically. It's very difficult sometimes to say no to people.

Leichtman: Do you think it's important for a psychic or medium to make it a practice to evaluate himself or herself?

Ford: Oh, yes. Every honest person needs to do that. And mediums and psychics, of all people, have to be scrupulously honest. Particularly with themselves! One of the first things a person who is developing psychic abilities should do is get to know himself well. In other words, mature self-awareness must precede psychic development.

Leichtman: Arthur, I've heard comments from individuals, who are in a position to be authoritative, stating flat-out in public that sometimes you did fudge a bit. They say that when you were good, you were very, very good, but there were times you apparently did cheat consciously.

Ford: No. That's the type of charge a dissatisfied customer usually makes about a psychic or medium, when he doesn't hear what he wanted to hear. It's also the kind of accusation jealous people make— people who can't stand the thought that someone

[26]

might be able to do competent psychic work on talent alone.

Leichtman: Yes, I know what you mean, and I'm sure a lot of psychics and mediums understand it, too.

Ford: If you don't mind, I'd like to pick up on some of the ideas Rosie and Fletcher talked about. I have spoken through David before, and it is a little easier for me than for some of the other spirits who are participating in this project. But before coming through, I had to go to Rosie, who taught me how to take care of David's body while I am using it—all the little foibles and problems.

Leadbeater had not quite graduated from Rosie's course when he first came through. She was very angry with him. I'm putting this in hyperbole, because I can't render it quite exactly. We do have to consult with the spirit guide of the medium before we can come in—otherwise, there would be certain problems. Any medium's body functions differently than the body we had in life.

Leichtman: Does David need extra energy when he's serving as a vehicle for spirits? If so, where does this energy come from?

Ford: Ah yes, I understand the question that is hidden in there. Let me give a little background on this subject first.

The essential power for me to come through David is an amalgam of the power of my being and the power of David's being. David is a somewhat frail physical specimen, but in terms of the psychic end of things, he's rather strong. I was in something of the same boat during the course of my career. I was somewhat frail physically but very strong psychically.

[27]

The source of this power is, of course, Universal Order, or God, or whatever label you would like to use. The power that is in all things, even spirits, comes from this source.

Now, some so-called ''mediums'' who are only slightly mediumistic depend on drawing their power from others sitting in the room in order to do their work. This is very unsanitary! It's not something any good medium would engage in. Of course, there is an energy transferral that goes on all the time between David and Colene [Mr. Johnson's wife] that does make it easier for us to work. Colene is aware of this and is quite freely involved in it. There is always an energy transferral between friends and close associates: this is correct and proper. It's a give-and-take situation. But when a medium draws energy out of everyone in the room just for his own well-being or power, not returning any of it, as many of these so-called mediums do it, then we have the image of the classic vampire [see glossary]. This is a very black state of affairs.

This problem is not limited just to psychic groups or psychic experiments, of course; it happens every day in stores and restaurants and public places all over the world. There are people who run around soaking up the basic energy of other people, because they haven't learned that the source of all power is Universal Order, God, or whatever you want to call it.

I hope this covers your hidden question.

Leichtman: Yes, very nicely. Before we get on to other things, I want to ask you to distinguish between mediumship and psychic ability. I'm talking now about what a person can do for himself versus what is a product of the efforts of a physical person plus his spooks.

Ford [*smiling*]: You certainly word things surreptitiously sometimes, don't you? [*Laughter.*]

Leichtman: I want to be very clear about it.

Ford: I understand. I'm trying to be a little less than stonewall sober this afternoon, because I think it's a mistake to pontificate. I reserve the right to inject a little levity here and there.

The best way to describe psychic ability is to give you some examples of its use. One would be having a premonition of danger, or, if you're trained, then all sorts of premonitions. Or, if you know how to do it, when the phone rings you know who's on the line before you pick up the receiver. This kind of awareness is done with your own inner sensitivity. It doesn't require the assistance of spirits.

Then there's clairvoyance. That's something you do with the visual receptors in your brain. Clairvoyant sight is perceived in the psychic body and then transmitted to these visual receptors. It's also something the psychic does for himself. He may have a little assistance from friends on the inner planes who come to teach him how to do it better. But he is essentially doing it himself with his own psychic mechanism. The psychic impulse works outward from the inner being in the form of a premonition, precognition, creative urge, or that sort of thing.

Mediumship is something else entirely. Mediums are not necessarily psychics. Psychics are not necessarily mediums. A medium is someone who has an extra faculty that he worked very hard to earn over the span of several lifetimes. It's an ability to step away from the physical personality and allow a spirit the medium trusts—in this case me—to use his mechanism of consciousness for a span of time.

Possession, by the way, is sometimes a case of a medium being used without his consent. He has lost control. A medium who is worth his salt controls the process because, after all, it is his body and his life. In this case, it's David's body and David's life. I would be imposing on him if I used his body longer than the span of time we've already agreed on—that is, the time that David's inner being and I have agreed on. David's spirit guides and guardians oversee this.

Mediumship is a pretty rare thing. There are quite a few excellent mediums around, but they're not nearly as numerous as those who presume the title. Anyone can close his eyes and allow his hysterical subconscious to put on a sheet and go, ''Boo, I'm a spook!'' [*Laughter*.] But he's only allowing his subconscious free reign.

There's a very delicate art to learning to open the back door of your subconscious for a being like me to come through and play the keyboard. Presuming to be a medium is not enough to prepare you to be one. Wishful thinking and pretense are no substitutes for the talent and hard work required.

Leichtman: I'm glad you mentioned that. Personally, I think it's very important for both mediums and psychics to honor what talent they have with hard work, intelligence, and responsibility. So many people assume that just going numb in the head is enough to get them going.

Ford: No, it actually gets them nowhere.

Leichtman [*drily*]: I've noticed that. [*Laughter*.] I

would like you to talk about the different degrees of trance involved in mediumship. Would it be possible, for example, for a medium in trance to walk around with his eyes open?

Ford: Oh, yes. You know, David has asked us not to open his eyes very often unless he is around people who are familiar with mediumship, and there are good reasons for this. If I were to open David's eyes, which I can do, the people sitting in the room would be a bit disconcerted by the fact that his eyes would be aimlessly rolling around and somewhat pink. Also, it's a bit hard on his eyes. I would not be looking through them, as I can see quite well through David's clairvoyant faculty. I have to use David's clairvoyance while I'm talking through him. My own being can see clairvoyantly, too, but not when I'm connected with David. I have to use his faculties.

David has at times opened his eyes slightly while in trance. As a matter of fact, I'm about to ask for a glass of water. Did you know that one time about five years ago Edgar Cayce was speaking through David and used David's body to make coffee at the same time? Several people found this very disturbing.

David is the kind of medium we don't have to take out into what is called a dead trance. He remains somewhat aware of what's going on, although he's not specifically aware of what I'm saying. He knows my intent but not the language I am using. Until he listens to the tape, he'll have almost no memory of what I'm saying, but David is in control of the situation. It's not a dead trance. He knows it's me sitting here—he can see me. He's off doing something else, but does keep an eye on the proceedings. He has given me the full use of his body; God forbid, but should there suddenly be a fire in the house, David wouldn't have to come running back to his body. I could get out the door with it. That's part of the agreement David has with his teachers and guides, because you never know. This particular kind of mediumship is easier on mediums, I think, than dead trance. It does tire him, but there are more safeguards, and David is in control. He gives me permission to use his body. This is a mature form of mediumship. Fletcher and I worked very much the same way.

This kind of arrangement also gives David certain experiences while he is out of his body. I can't relate where he's standing at the moment to this room, because where he is standing is not related to the room. It's hard to explain, but David has an opportunity, while he's out of his body during trance, to learn and gain experiences on the inner planes. Often, this opportunity to learn is directly related to the material being given in the seance. That makes him a more useful part of the whole process.

The advantage of this type of trance is that, in the proper circumstances and with the right medium, it can be used to communicate pure ideas at a preverbal level. The spirit does this by projecting abstract thoughts into the mind of the medium. It's the medium, then, who translates the ideas into actual words.

Leichtman: But that sounds like more work for the medium.

Ford: Yes, but it allows a spirit such as Chikamatsu [the Japanese dramatist Chikamatsu Monzaemon, who appeared with William Shakespeare in *Shakespeare Returns*], who does not know English, to speak through David and carry on an intelligent conversation with you.

Then there is what is called the dead trance, which is sometimes a bit dangerous. There aren't many mediums who are able to control it fully. That's because mediumship, unfortunately, has often attracted people who are not too intelligent—people who are not using logic, who are not thoughtful or careful. These are people who just want attention. Usually the real purpose of going into a dead trance is to manifest ectoplasm. There are some occasions when this has to be done, but it can be extremely dangerous to the health of the medium. David has taken part in a couple of experiments in which he developed about three gallons of ectoplasm and then had to go to bed for two days because he was so tired. Nothing ever came of it.

A medium would have to go into a dead trance to make a table fly through the air, or anything similar. These are extremely exhausting experiences, because something of the medium's physical strength has to be used to produce the ectoplasm, whether or not the body or the personality is directly involved.

One of the main advantages of the dead trance is that it does give the spirit near-total control of the medium's body. This allows the spirit to use his own voice, speech patterns, and gestures—not the words and mannerisms of the medium. Even though it is dangerous, the dead trance is valuable at times, because the messages that come through can be remarkably impressive and convincing. There are recorded cases, for example, of spirits speaking in obscure foreign dialects, unknown to the medium, but perfectly understandable to relatives attending the seance.

The weakness of this type of trance is that it is very limited. I wish more people would understand that and not insist that *all* mediums must produce this type of phenomena in order to prove themselves genuine. In many ways, the lighter trance is much more versatile than the dead trance.

Then there is another kind of trance I'm sure you and several others here in the room have experienced, although you may not think of it as a trance. This a condition in which you find yourself saying something that you know did not come out of your own mind. It's a very light state, and can be maintained indefinitely without being too wearing. I believe you work in this state frequently when you're typing. David types with Dr. Kammutt [an inner planes teacher who works with both Dr. Leichtman and Mr. Johnson] half the day and is not terribly fatigued—except that his chair gets awfully tired. [*Laughter.*]

Fletcher wants me to add here that there is a lot of nonsense making the rounds at the moment relating trance to hypnosis. A lot of people talk loosely about ''hypnotic trance.'' Actually, the word ''trance'' was originally used to describe a medium's state of consciousness. When hypnosis became popular, the word was borrowed and used to describe the mesmerized state as well, because people thought it was similar to the mediumistic trance. The use of this one word to describe two very different states of mind has caused much confusion.

The important point to remember about the different levels of trance is that the usefulness of the medium depends on his or her talent and intelligence, not the depth or style with which he or she works. The other significant factor affecting the quality of a communication is the integrity of both the medium and the spirit using the channel.

Mrs. Garrett [Eileen Garrett, whose interview will be the eleventh in this series] would like to talk more at length about this subject than I care to today.

Leichtman: Is it correct to conclude from your comments that psychic ability is *not* totally dependent upon one's clairaudient capacity to hear some spook?

Ford: No, psychic ability is not at all dependent upon listening to a spirit. This *can* be part of it, but the range of a psychic is not restricted to this one phenomenon alone. There are many things a psychic can do for himself. Always remember that a psychic is also a spirit in physical form, and it's therefore possible for him to get in touch with his own spirit. In fact, this is more frequently what a psychic does—particularly the creative psychic, such as an artist or a musician. He is listening to his own inner being. He is not necessarily contacting a famous musician of the past and receiving dictations of music, although that can happen. Schubert, I understand, has been doing a very good job lately with a lady in England named Rosemary Brown [the author of *Unfinished Symphonies* and *Immortals By My Side*]. Those melodies were burning in his head when he died, and he never got a chance to write them down. He's very pleased to have this opportunity.

Leichtman: All right. To change the subject a bit but to pick up a topic that's been discussed by others in this project, do you have any ideas you would care to share about the current state of occult literature?

Ford: Books on psychic and occult matters are very popular nowadays, and they sell well, but many of them aren't very original or worth much. Let's take the subject of palmistry, for the sake of argument. There are certain authors who will quite literally get together all the books they can on the subject of palmistry and then copy a paragraph out of this one and a paragraph out of that one and put all the paragraphs together and publish it as an ''original'' book. If you looked at a group of books on any occult subject, you'd find that many of them are just copies of other books—and copied by a person who did not understand what he was writing. Perhaps he used fancier pictures and diagrams, but essentially he didn't understand what he was doing. That's a major source of confusion in the literature of today.

Then there are authors who are more psychotic than psychic. [*Laughter.*] That adds to the confusion.

Leichtman: How can the average reader separate the wheat from the chaff?

Ford: Well, his basic approach to reading is very important. Unfortunately, most people read largely to reaffirm their old beliefs, rather than to stimulate their minds with new and perhaps challenging ideas. As a reader comes across an idea he finds provocative, he should honor its potential and experiment with it in his own life—and in this way determine its value to him. If the idea doesn't work for him, then he should discard it and go on to another idea. This is the only rational and safe way a person can proceed.

People would do well to remember also that in most real occult work there is a safety valve. If someone is reading without discrimination, he'll get caught up in the process of puzzling over the seeming discrepancies of what he's reading, until he gets lost in a maze of half-logic. As a result, he never gets to work with the substance of the ideas he's dealing with—until he's prepared himself to handle them.

When you're reading a book, it would be good if you tried to fit it into what you already know; parts that don't fit in should be experimented with. Plan to read an occult book rather slowly; too many people try to rush through from beginning to end immediately.

David started by reading St. Theresa; I started on something equally abstruse—St. John of the Cross. Those weren't the easiest writings to digest—I remember one of them taking me five years to read and understand! And of course there were many books that, as I reread them later, I found I no longer agreed with them, because I had come to know better. You can only go by experience. Books and conversations are good for giving you ideas you can try out, but unless you can prove something yourself, you should discard it.

Leichtman: Didn't you once suggest checking very carefully the authority of the author when selecting a book?

Ford: Yes, but sometimes the author's authority is not always a recommendation for a book. Some of the doctors, for example, who write about psychic phenomena aren't writing from personal experience, but by observing others and then making theories about how they *think* it works. These are just intellectual exercises; their theories are constructed out of nothing more than straw and tinker toys. They add nothing of value to the occult literature.

Leichtman: They're not really authorities, then.

Ford: No, because they lack first-hand knowledge.

Leichtman: In other words, a reader should look for books by authors who are competent because of their own experience and wisdom, not for books by half-baked scientists or people who merely report what they have observed.

Ford: Or some sensationally-worded, gaudy paperback.

Leichtman: Yes. Another question I want to ask concerns the Sun Moon commentaries you made.

Ford: What is it you would like to know about Sun Moon?

Leichtman: Number one, I wasn't clear whether this man was a spirit or in the physical at the time you did those sittings in 1964.

Ford: That information got garbled, and I'm afraid I have to plead a little guilty. My author friend and I decided we would have to proceed on that particular series of ideas with a bit of caution. It was intentionally garbled. And, while I want to clear it up a bit, I'm afraid the record even now must remain a bit garbled: that's the nature of the thing. When that information came through, it startled me tremendously. I was a bit afraid of the whole thing, and at a loss as to what to do with it. There again—to go back to the conversation about preparing for a sitting—I was completely unprepared to handle that situation adequately. I might add that it was only with great reluctance that this material was added to the book.

Those sittings were done at the request of a Mr. Sun Myung Moon [a Korean evangelist who founded the Unification Church] who is now running around the country getting converts. Fletcher used the occasion to drop some hints in a symbolic way, but a careful reading of what he said will reveal that he never endorsed this particular person, even though Mr. Moon's followers have tried to get mileage out of the statements made. And the hints that were dropped had nothing to do with Sun Myung Moon. Neither Fletcher nor I endorse anything that this man has done.

Leichtman: Can you elaborate some more on the hints Fletcher dropped?

Ford: Yes, but I must still be oblique about it.

There is at this time, and you have some awareness of this, developing a man who will become as the Christ of this age. Many of us who have gotten information on this, and have published material on it, intentionally garbled it to protect the person who is going to do this important work. This is because there are so many people willing to volunteer for the position! What is it—forty-five second comings of the Christ that you and David have run into already? Last Saturday night David met the forty-sixth one! All I can say, Colene, is God help us if *he* becomes the Christ! [*Laughter.*] And there will be more of this sort of thing happening, because humanity is vaguely aware that something momentous is about to transpire.

The real man I'm talking about *is* living. He is above the age of reason and can vote and make decisions for himself, but it is not yet time for him to start his ministry. When he does, things are going to be difficult enough for him without a lot of prior advertising. Look now at the people who claim to be Jesus Christ. All you can do is laugh and say, ''Oh, God help us!'' The man I'm talking about is going to encounter problems of this nature—except that he is going to come in a very unusual way. The events are not going to be similar to the career of Jesus and the start of His ministry.

Actually, the phrase "Sun Moon" creates a good mental picture, although this is *not* the real name of the avatar. It's like a dial code or telephone number. People who have studied advanced astrology might find a bit of a clue here, but it will not give them the name or whereabouts of the gentleman, so it's safe to mention.

[*Accepting a glass of water*] Thank you. David has a dry mouth.

Leichtman: Is there anything else you wanted to say about Sun Moon?

Ford: Yes. That little episode does demonstrate one of the problems that can occasionally arise in mediumship. Sometimes the people who come to a seance are so fanatical and set in their expectations of what they want to hear that they can actually intimidate the medium psychically—without the medium knowing it. You must remember that a medium is in a passive, receptive state while he's doing his work. That makes him very vulnerable to exceptionally strong thoughts and feelings directed at him. Sometimes the spirit in charge cannot completely keep those thoughts out of the communication. That's one of the problems that occurred in the Sun Moon sessions.

Leichtman: Yes, fanaticism can poison consciousness at levels deeper than many people suspect.

Ford: The reason you're seeing so many second comings of Jesus, second comings of Buddha, and even the rise of black magic and Satanism, is because humanity is vaguely aware that something big is going to happen. When someone says, ''Oh, I'm Mary Magdalene,'' or ''I'm Jesus,'' this is just a very strange response to genuine impelling forces. Humanity is tuning in, more or less consciously, to these particular forces coming from within, from the inner planes, at this time. This is one of the reasons why there is such a rise in the interest in psychic phenomena, after all—because we are all making ready for the reappearance of the Christ. Jesus only had one harbinger, but the Christ of the New Age is going to have several million harbingers.

As you know, several of the people who were associated with Jesus during His life have now reincarnated. They don't advertise it, but these people are genuine.

Leichtman: Yes.

Ford: Before you giggle too hard when someone says she's Mary Magdalene, stop and consider that this is really a symptom of something very wonderful about to happen, whether or not that person actually was Mary Magdalene. And it might be uplifting for her to think so, particularly if she is tapping into the consciousness of the mature Mary Magdalene. She may learn something. Someone like Mary Magdalene or the Madonna or any of the cast of characters of that lifetime (again, I'm being a bit facetious) can momentarily overshadow someone to the point where he thinks he is a reincarnation of that person.

Madame Blavatsky is telling me about a lady who thinks she is an incarnation of her. She says this is all very well and good, because she is working with that lady. The lady is so in rapport with H.P.B. that it is an honest mistake, you see. She is learning something from the experience. We get our work done in very mysterious ways sometimes.

Now, in what I've just been saying lies the real hint for why Fletcher chose to say what he did in the Sun Myung Moon sittings. And there's a tie-in here with some of the ideas Cheiro mentioned about the synchronicity of the universe in his interview.

Harry White: What kind of role do you see the new avatar performing?

Ford: I'm going to have to condense a very complicated set of ideas in order to answer that. Whenever there has been an avatar, there has been a lifting of the vibration of the whole human race. You can look for that and much more. The physical plane is rapidly moving into the fourth dimension. Part of the avatar's work is to raise the consciousness of the planet so that this particular transition can be made. That is the first thing that will happen.

You're going to be noticing within your lifetimes that some things aren't working quite like they used to, and this will be an indication that this transition is happening. At the same time, there will be an increasing awareness of some of the inhabitants of the finer side of life—entities such as elves, angels, and spooks. This will be another indication of what is happening.

The major work of the coming avatar is to lay the foundation for a truly spiritual civilization based on a clarification of the ancient wisdom and a new revelation. He will guide us up the next evolutionary step for mankind, which is basically what every avatar comes to do.

White: Will he work in the traditional church?

Ford: I don't think he will be working through the framework of traditional Christianity any more than Jesus Christ worked through the traditional framework of Judaism. He will probably have his beginnings there, because that will be the predominant religion of whatever community he is in. However, I'm sure he will go beyond it. We forget that Buddha began in the Hindu religion and broke through the traditional framework for that and created something new, too.

Leichtman: All right. I can't use the colloquialism that you're "dying to say something," but I know that you are eager to talk about the need to put psychic phenomena back into the church.

Ford: Yes, I am. In my lifetime I had the opportunity to talk to many church leaders in the United States and elsewhere about the mystical experience, and that pleased me a great deal. Hopefully, the mystical experience is the end result of the psychic experience, and this means that the psychic experience does have its place in the church and in religion. By religion I don't necessarily mean organized churches.

The ideas we generated in these conversations with church leaders led to the building up of an organization known as the Spiritual Frontiers Fellowship, which is still going, although I'm not sure at the moment that it's doing too much to promote the basic ideals that got it started.

Most of the early pagan churches, as well as the Jewish religion, depended on oracles and psychics of one sort or another. They thought of their mediums as the mouthpieces of God, and essentially they were. Most of the ancient religions were built up around these people and their sayings. The Hebrew religion, after all, depended for its knowledge of God upon its prophets. Even Christianity was built upon this foundation.

The prophets, you know, were a type of medium who did not like the word "medium" any more than I liked it in my lifetime, or any more than David likes it. The word has connotations of some kind of gross, fat lady with too much makeup and too many beads, sitting in a dingy room with a crystal ball. [*Laughter.*] Yes, those types of people were around even in ancient times. So the prophets and seers and sibyls all invented their own names, so they wouldn't be associated with the other type of medium.

I want to state at this point that there is a great deal of difference in the quality of the psychic and mediumistic abilities of various people. A lot depends on the consciousness of the psychic or medium. If the person is earnestly seeking to grow and develop and do something constructive with what he's been given, chances are that something more or less important will be given to him to relate to others. On the other hand, a lot of out-and-out frauds also get into this sort of thing. And, there are some people who want attention and happen to be slightly psychic or mediumistic. These people will entertain whatever spook comes to them, without regard for the nature of the consciousness of the spirit. Or, they take whatever psychic impression comes to them and run with it, without regard for the quality of the ideas they are getting.

This is meant to be just an outline form. The high end of the scale of psychic or mediumistic ability is the capacity to tap into the roots of mysticism. This involves some kind of rapport with the Order of the universe—an understanding of it and a participation with it. When you view psychic ability from this perspective, then you begin to see that it should never really be used for ''parlor game'' effects—which form the low end of the scale.

The ancients had very rigorous tests for the psychics and mediums that worked in the temples. This was true even of the Jewish people of that remote period. But it's not hard to spot the frauds: a sensible person can see them by himself, just by looking at the quality of the reading he gets. Unfortunately, it seems that many people don't ever get around to *looking* for the frauds, let alone *seeing* them.

The Christian Church came to life within the context of the pagan world, which is something Christians nowadays seem to forget. Christianity began in a world that was essentially pagan. There were many, many religions at that time. Some religions recognized, among other gods, the god of the Christians. One Roman set up an altar in Rome to the ''unknown god,'' because he could never find out the name of the Jewish god. Be that as it may, the tradition of the psychic and the oracle in the temple was still quite alive, and a valuable part of the culture.

Quite naturally, some of these psychics and oracles became Christians, because they could see the value of the growing Christian church—which was very much unlike the modern Christian church, incidentally. An early Christian meeting—before the Church was recognized as the official religion of Rome—was a meeting something like this group gathered here today. It was a group of people who got together to share their religious and spiritual and psychic experiences. The group members shared their growth in all these things and helped each other. In the early days, these groups were frequently begun either by one of the disciples of Jesus or by one of their followers. They would sit with the group several times and get it started thinking in the perspective of Christianity. Then, when the group was on its feet, they would appoint someone to lead the group, and move on.

Up until about the middle of the tenth century almost every such group developed at least one or two psychics. In the days of Paul, for example, the Christian Church taught psychics to participate in the religious services much in the way a priest of minister does today, but with the added ability of being a psychic, too. Paul's letter to the Church of Corinth in the New Testament is about just this kind of development. He had apparently visited the people there and helped the church get its classes set up and organized. Then he went on to somewhere else and later received a report that the Corinthians were playing parlor games with their psychic abilities and doing the other kinds of things we see in some of our modern circles. ''Oh, you were Julius Caeser,'' or ''You were Cleopatra''—that sort of thing. [*Laughter.*] Of course, these things are really foolish in the long run: when you have an experience in which you remember that you have lived forever, you don't need to play these parlor games anymore. So Paul wrote back to the Church of Corinth and said (I am paraphrasing): ''Don't make a parlor game out of something sacred! Use it for something important!'' Now, there's an injunction that more modern psychics ought to take to heart—*use it for the most important purpose you can think of!*

It shocks a lot of modern Christians to learn that psychic abilities were always intended to be a part of the church service, and a part of the work of the church and religious groups. It also shocks modern Christians to learn about the idea of reincarnation. Why should that be so shocking? All through the Bible and other Christian teachings we're told that we live forever. So why are ''Christians'' so surprised when someone can come up with proof of that by psychically recalling previous lives, or by mediumistically speaking with the so-called ''dead''? Why do so many ''Christians'' think it's something evil to be able to prove what the Bible says is true? I don't understand peoples' present attitudes, although I do understand them in a historical light.

My argument is this: why shouldn't someone who is a bit closer to the ear of God than others in the congregation of a church—why shouldn't this person participate in the service of the church? I don't mean to pontificate, but it seems to me that this would make religion a great deal more meaningful for most people. This very human talent of being able to listen to angels is certainly something that ought to be back in religion where it belongs.

If there was more acceptance of the psychic and the medium in the modern church, there would be a lot less foolishness in these areas today. And some of the foolishness is really surprising. For instance, some of the ''New Thought'' churches accept psychics up to a certain point, but won't go beyond that. They just won't discuss some of the higher possibilities of the psychic experience, and they won't train mediums in the church. The ministers of these churches will freely consult mediums, but they won't give them a religious framework in which to study, develop, work, and prosper. This is a very bad situation, because the developing medium must then go out and find whatever teacher and support he can, and the teacher may not have any kind of religious inclination.

There is one group of churches that has overdone the psychic angle to a rather hysterical degree. They embrace any spook who announces himself as such and regard him in great awe—whether he deserves it or not. They get involved in a great deal of foolishness, holding seances conducted by people who don't know their ectoplasm from their elbow and certifying people as mediums without giving them proper training.

This is the other extreme and isn't any more desirable than the first. What I'd like to see lies in between. Modern organized religion has got to take a serious look at psychic phenomena and evaluate it in a new light. Even the inner circle of the Roman Catholic Church accepts the mysteries and its attendant psychic phenomena. Of course, they don't teach it to the laity at all. They keep it behind closed doors with their "in-group" and make no effort to use psychic phenomena to help members of the congregation lift their sight. Have I made this clear, Doctor, or is it getting muddled?

Leichtman: No, it's very clear. Is the Christian Church in any way moving in these directions— toward a greater acceptance of immortality, spiritual healing, and psychic phenomena?

Ford: I think the world at large is.

Leichtman: Do you think the world at large is ahead of the Christian Church in its acceptance of these things?

Ford: Yes. Christianity, like all religions, is mystical in nature, yet many people overlook this fact. I ask you: how many Christians are ever taught about the mystery of their own religion? It's there for someone who is very astute to find for himself, but most people are not astute enough to find it in the literature or the teachings given them. And certainly this dimension of Christianity is never clearly stated by any of the teachers of modern, organized religion.

A mystic is a person who has had a large number of psychic experiences, but these experiences are of the type that reveal to him that nature is ordered, alive, and governed by something that's very wise and benevolent. The mystic goes through a phase in which he becomes intimately aware that the other creatures of the planet are also part of this life and share in this same order. He learns that he can communicate with these creatures, not just cats and dogs and horses but also roses and daisies and all the rest. He realizes that there is a brotherhood of mankind, too. These realizations *are* psychic experiences, albeit psychic experiences that differ vastly from the usual work of a psychic reader.

It's quite possible for us—if we raise our sights—to communicate with all these forms of life, because it is One Life. It is One Life that is working very hard to make the parts of It cooperate, and the parts are very aware of each other. But we human beings, having the great logical gift that has been given to us, sometimes talk ourselves right out of participating with it.

It would do a great deal for the moral fiber of modern man to know these things—*but to know them from his own experiences!*

Yet a mystic goes beyond just understanding and tries to participate in some way in this One Life and to work actively with Its ordered purpose—both with his inner being and his outer being as well. This participation is essentially psychic. And so, it's not just cats and dogs and roses that the mystic is aware of, but also many people on the inner planes, and angels, and all the life of the inner worlds. He may never know his friends on the inner planes by name; he may never have given them a label. Perhaps he doesn't care to; he may trust them as they are, without a label. But through his inner being, he has these contacts.

A psychic may or may not be a mystic. However, it is hoped that as someone begins to have psychic experiences, he will reach out for a higher, mystical realization. Anyway, this is what I talked about to many, many ministers when I was in life. I think I left, with some of them at least, an understanding that mysticism must be more openly discussed, thought about, and investigated in organized religious circles. I hope this movement toward mysticism will continue.

Now, what questions are burning in your mind?

Leichtman: What about the role of healing in the church?

Ford: Many churches in their ordinary services do pray for the sick, but much, much more could be done. The reality of spiritual healing has already been abundantly demonstrated. Let's not forget that one of the principal features of the ministry of Jesus was healing. And it wasn't just Jesus—his disciples and those who followed also healed. This is well recorded in the New Testament. Healing was a prominent part of the work of the early Christian Church. It's sad more ''Christians'' don't appreciate the historical tradition of healing in their own religion. And it's a shame that ministers and priests don't recognize that healing is a *duty* of their office.

The gift of healing has never been absent from the human race. It's always been quietly and informally practiced by spiritually dedicated and compassionate people in all walks of life. In modern times, it's not uncommon to find people using this gift in such activities as nursing, medicine, psychology, social work, and parenting. There's no reason why some of these good people cannot be welcomed by the church as lay assistants in healing services.

More healing needs to be done in the churches. After all, a demonstration of healing is part of what religion is all about. The real source of life in the universe is God—and when God manifests, it shouldn't be as a pompous sermon or an elaborate ritual so much as something that will *benefit people*. It should inspire the congregation, lift them up, heal their ignorance, soothe their fears, and mend their bodies.

Leichtman: Oh, very good. A while ago, you said that you weren't sure if the Spiritual Frontiers Fellowship was living up to its original ideals. Do you want to elaborate on that? Has it turned out the way—

Ford: No, it hasn't turned out the way I wanted it to. I was hoping that Spiritual Frontiers would bring psychic awareness into the church for a fuller involvement with religion. Instead, they seem to be playing party games. Teaching things like the I Ching is not exactly what I had hoped and worked for.

Leichtman: Well, there seems to be a tremendous interest in healing throughout the country, and Spiritual Frontiers certainly is giving a lot of time and attention to that.

Ford: The SFF probably does attract some good healers, but I imagine most of them get disgusted with the party games and go on to other things. A lot of good mediums are lost in the same way, too.

Leichtman: Do you think Spiritual Frontiers, as an organization, is terminally ill?

Ford: No, but I'm really very disappointed. The people who in effect steer the organization are lacking in vision. They are not implementing the ideals on which the organization is founded. And they haven't succeeded in getting the interest of the ministers and the churches. Instead, it's become just another occult organization. By default, perhaps by design, it has lapsed into a lay organization devoted to party games. It needs to restore its emphasis on the mystical experience and forget the flashy fringes of psychic phenomena. Only then will it be attractive to the churches.

I guess what I'm saying is that it needs to do a healing on itself.

Leichtman: If you were here in the physical, Arthur, and could make specific recommendations, what would you suggest as a way to correct the situation? What should the leadership be doing? What should the members of SFF be doing?

Ford: Both the leaders and the members should stand up and call for a return to the original intent of SFF. They should work to clean out the foolishness—and the fools. No doubt this will require a great deal of courage, but courage is an essential part of the spiritual life.

Leichtman: Sounds like a tall order.

Ford: I'm willing to grant that it's easier said than done. But it must be done.

If it's all right with you, I'd like to switch places with Fletcher for awhile, and let him talk.

Leichtman: Okay.

Ford: I'll be back.

[*There followed a pause, while Arthur withdrew from Mr. Johnson's body, and Fletcher stepped in.*]

Leichtman: Welcome back.

Fletcher: I didn't really leave, you know. I've been listening to everything you and Arthur have been talking about. You have quite a little audience on the inner planes today.

Leichtman: Arthur was just mentioning the party games in psychic circles. What happens when psychics and mediums start indulging in hanky-panky—or just get sloppy? How do the spirits trying to work through them deal with that?

Fletcher: What makes you think we would want to deal with that type of medium or psychic? For that matter, why would a physical person want to? If a client did come to such a medium, needing guidance he couldn't get any other way, one of us could probably shove some advice through. But ordinarily, we would not bother.

If someone fudges intentionally and habitually, eventually the mediumistic door is shut for good. This is not a decision that I or anybody else makes. There's really no decision to it: it just happens automatically. That's the way universal order works.

Hopefully, all mediums and psychics would be making an effort to grow spiritually, as well as refine their psychic skills. Whenever that's the case, they would obviously be developing greater integrity, a broader sense of responsibility, and a deeper respect for Truth. For such a person, the problems of hanky-panky and cheating would not be relevant.

Leichtman: What can you say about the effects of deceit and cheating?

Fletcher: Under the law of karma, you get what you send out. The more anyone cheats and lies and steals, the more he opens himself up to being cheated, to being lied to, and to being stolen from.

Leichtman: That makes sense.

Fletcher: And even experiences in prison.

Leichtman: Do you mean a literal prison?

Fletcher: Yes. Now, before anybody misinterprets these comments, I should say that there are mediums and psychics who are beginning to practice their craft who do get sophomoric and think they know more than they do. As a result, they may make *honest* mistakes. But this doesn't necessarily mean that they are cheating.

Unfortunately, a lot of people think that the business of being a psychic or a medium is very glamorous; actually, it's not. Many people with only a little ability get into the work, and find they thoroughly enjoy all the attention they're getting—and money, too, sometimes. Sometimes they get to be well-known too early in their career; the demand is great, and they're not properly developed, and that overtaxes what small abilities they have. As a consequence, they burn themselves out.

Leichtman: Psychically?

Fletcher: They can even develop physical problems.

Leichtman: Mmm. May I go on to something else?

Fletcher: Oh, please do. [*Laughter.*]

Leichtman: How should the public treat the psychics and mediums they consult?

Fletcher: Well, certainly with the same courtesy with which they would treat anyone else. Obviously, good manners are always important, but they are exceptionally important when you are dealing with someone who is psychically sensitive. Your attitudes and behavior affect the psychic's capacity to do good work. After all, a climate of rudeness not only poisons social relationships, but it also poisons psychic relationships.

Many people come to a psychic because they have a need, but at the same time, they often have a feeling in the back of their minds that the psychic is doing something evil. And so they treat the psychic in this light. Sometimes they actually lie, and that creates an even greater barrier against getting a good result in the reading.

Leichtman: Is there anything you would like to say about the reports that you and Arthur had some philosophical differences?

Fletcher: That's not uncommon at all. We are two entirely different individuals.

Leichtman [*chuckling*]: Imagine that.

Fletcher: If everybody were the same, it would be a very boring world, don't you think?

Leichtman: It would be worse than that! I know I have my differences with my friends in spirit.

Fletcher: Gosh, if someone thinks that just because a spirit doesn't have a physical body he can't have his own ideas, they're wrong.

Leichtman: I take it, then, that there can be differences that do not impair the overall psychic connection or the overall function.

Fletcher: Well, it's just like on a job, actually. You work alongside people you disagree with—and yet you get the job done.

Leichtman: Well, let me ask this: what kind of work are you engaged in now, since you're no longer coming through Arthur?

Fletcher: I'm coming through David. [*Laughter.*]

Leichtman: That's not full-time work, though. What else are you doing?

Fletcher: I'm working with a group of physical children, helping them retain their psychic abilities.

Leichtman: That's fascinating. I'd like to follow up on it. If some interested, compassionate parent has a child that seems to be psychic, what should he be doing to help the child preserve his psychic abilities?

Fletcher: For one thing, adults ought to allow children to have active imaginations. They ought to help the child understand that being psychic is part of a natural phenomenon. It doesn't make them special. It is simply a talent that they have. Unfortunately, a lot of *adults* who have developed psychic abilities haven't learned that lesson yet.

Growing up is always difficult, but it's especially important for a psychic child to be raised in an atmosphere of support and love, so they develop a healthy self-image and confidence.

Leichtman: Would you advise parents to caution children not to talk about their psychic experiences?

Fletcher: It should be explained to them that this

isn't something that you talk about with everybody. If a parent carefully explains to a child that certain topics might scare some people, then the child will be able to understand the value of this restraint, and not get into trouble.

Leichtman: Are these children likely to be more sensitive to criticism, or more emotional?

Fletcher: They're going to be more sensitive in general. However, they'll tend to be more comfortable with many things that disturb adults. For example, children are apt to strike up friendships with spirits very quickly.

Leichtman: Is there a need to discuss ethics with such psychic children—the need to be discreet or the need to respect other people's privacy?

Fletcher: Oh, yes. Also, parents should never exploit the child's ability for their own ends. Just like stage mothers, a lot of parents of psychic children drag them around to do predictions and things. This isn't appropriate.

Leichtman: Would it be useful for the parents to guide these psychically-gifted children into creative activities and hobbies, as a means of focussing their psychic ability?

Fletcher: Definitely. All of these things should be encouraged.

Leichtman: Are there books you could recommend to parents to read that might help them raise such children? I'm thinking, for example, of a classic called, *The Boy Who Saw True.*

Fletcher: Yes, that's very good.

Leichtman: It's a book about the early life of a boy that was clairvoyant from birth, and what happened to him. It might help parents understand what psychic children go through.

Fletcher: *Kinship With All Life* would be enlightening, too.

Leichtman: Yes. Some parents have the notion that every psychic person is destined to turn out to be another Edgar Cayce or another Jeane Dixon or another friendly fortune teller—

Fletcher: Well, of course that isn't true. You'd be surprised at the number of people in this town [Carmel, California] who are very psychic but don't do readings for people. Instead, they use their talents to better their lives and the lives of the people around them. As a matter of fact, there are a number of business people in town who have a great deal of psychic ability, know it, and use it.

Leichtman: In that case, I suppose reading something like *Breakthrough to Creativity* by Shafica Karagulla would be useful.

Fletcher: Yes.

Leichtman: Anything else you would like to add?

Fletcher: No, I don't think I can add anything. Arthur is eager to talk to you again.

Leichtman: Okay. Thank you for coming.

[*Fletcher then withdrew, permitting Arthur Ford to resume use of the medium.*]

Ford: Since in life I was a medium, there are a couple of observations I'd like to make about the need for common sense. It's good to be able to hear voices and do this and that psychically, but there also has to be a measure for the validity of all this. When someone believes he may be psychic, he must take care not to launch his explorations into the psychic realms unless he first arms himself with large amounts of common sense and caution.

If a voice spoke to you, saying, "I am your master teacher and I tell you to do so and so and then, after you've done that, run your car off the cliff," you would dismiss that "spirit" rather quickly, because the advice does not make particularly good sense. If *any* spirit came in and *ordered* me to do anything, I would reply, "You're not the kind of teacher I need," because a real spiritual teacher does not order. Spooks have no right to command physical people, any more than you have the right to command one another.

If you get any psychic impression that you don't fully understand, don't act upon it until you do. Wait and see what it means first. If you're puzzled about anything, you should put it in a little suspense file over here [*indicating a region of David's mind*], until you see how it all will work out. Then, after a period of time, you'll begin to understand it.

I found it very difficult to think of myself as a medium in the beginning, but I began to see that the messages coming through, the understandings I was gaining, and the experiences I was having were genuine; I could rely on them. And I came to learn that Fletcher was always going to be honest with me. But I proceeded with a great deal of caution and care—I didn't immediately jump into something just because Fletcher told me to.

This leads me to another thought, which I suppose is one of your pet ideas, too. There is a great deal of difference among spooks, so it's important to determine what kind of spook you may be communicating with. This is done very much like making a new friend in the physical. How do you know what kind of person someone is? You wait and see and proceed with caution. After a period of time, you begin to know whether you can trust what he says and does. It's the same in striking up friendships with spooks—or should be.

The gamut of spirits is more extensive than some people imagine. It starts with little elementals who can sometimes speak a bit of English, although it's like baby talk. But they are very primitive and unintelligent and can be harmful. Another kind of spirit you can run into—one of a slightly higher order—is your own subconscious. Your subconscious is a very willing servant of your logical mind. So, if you desperately want to hear from a spirit, the subconscious is quite willing to pretend to be one. But if you are in the habit of filing everything that happens to you for awhile until you learn what's going on, you won't be deceived. You'll see very soon that it's just your subconscious trying to satisfy you.

Of course, many members of the spirit world are human beings that have passed over. But keep in mind that there's a great deal of difference among humans, too. I had a relative who was a very nice person but he had not been able to finish the third grade, because he didn't have the mental equipment to understand what he had been taught in the third grade. He was a little pathetic but a very nice person—a very honest person. Well, he passed over, and then somebody suggested that I contact him about a financial deal that a friend and I were involved in at the time. This relative was certainly the last person I would have asked that kind of question while he was alive; nor would there have been any point in asking him just because he had passed over. He would not have changed that much. Do you see what I'm driving at?

Leichtman: Yes.

Ford: By contrast, in David's life along came Rosie, just as Fletcher had come along in my life. Rosie was bubbly and giggly and carried on, yet she also started telling him things that were intelligent and true—and outside his ordinary range of understanding. And he suddenly realized that this lady was a wise friend who had come to help him.

Of course, the gamut goes on through teachers and masters and on and on *ad infinitum.* A psychic needs to be very careful about distinguishing among spirits. God gave humanity a great gift: God gave us minds. We are not meant to suspend our intelligence just because we are investigating some spook. We must evaluate whatever comes through.

Leichtman: Do you have something more specific to say about what type of psychic ability should be used in the church, besides giving out messages from dead relatives and simple prophecy?

Ford: Seeking messages from dead relatives has a purpose for the bereaved. People frequently need the reassurance that their deceased loved ones are alive and well somewhere. It certainly does have value, but it's a kind of limited value. A medium that would settle for this kind of work alone is not properly honoring his talent.

The "message service" in the Spiritualist Church (and others) is really not a service at all. The relay of messages from the dead is something that should be done in private and it should be brief—just so the bereaved will know that their relatives are alive and well.

So what should be the role of psychic phenomena in church services? Well, there's a whole range of possibilities that *enlightened* psychics could explore. I would not want to limit it just to healing, for example. The value of the higher aspects of psychic ability and phenomena is absolutely enormous, mainly because this type of extended awareness can bring into our understanding the hidden nature of God. A large measure of the hidden life of God stands revealed to well trained and enlightened psychics. Obviously, I'm not talking about the type of psychic who tells fortunes for lovesick ladies or men. I'm talking about someone who, because of his training and spiritual instincts, seeks to explore the phenomena of life, the nature of God, and how God relates to the physical plane. These issues are the proper study of any enlightened psychic, and greatly enhance the religious life.

Now, to be specific, a psychic can perceive the aura which surrounds every living thing—human, animal, and plant—and can also perceive the factors that affect the aura, that can harm the aura, and also those that can heal the aura. In many churches, they talk a lot about the need for positive thinking and the danger of negative thinking. Well, the psychic can see the evidence for this. The psychic can see and talk authoritatively about the cleansing value of prayer and the healing properties of effective meditation. This can greatly support the belief and efforts of the congregation.

Leichtman: These aren't things to be taken solely on faith, then?

Ford: Well, that's the whole point. The enlightened psychic can actually see what most other people *have* to take on faith. He can report back in detail, not just that there is survival of the personality after death, but that Uncle John and Aunt Alice are really quite alive over here, they look well, and they are now healed of the cancer or stroke that killed their physical body, and have started a whole new life on the inner planes. No, it's not necessary to take these matters on faith at all. One can, as Paul admonished everyone, add *understanding* to our faith.

Leichtman: Are you suggesting, then, that the apostles and prophets didn't take these things on faith? They could actually see them? And it would be valuable for people now to do the same?

Ford: Oh, of course. All of the named disciples in the New Testament were obviously highly-evolved souls, and they all had a good measure of spiritual intuition and discernment. It would have been impossible for them to have been accepted by Jesus unless they had such refined awareness. This awareness is something that every religious person, every mystic, and every student on the Path eventually must attain, and I'll tell you the reason why. For one thing, this awareness gives the individual *direct, mystical contact* with things of the spirit, such as angels. Now, doesn't this direct contact sound better than faith alone?

Leichtman: Of course. As Paul said, ''I believe, but I *know* what I believe in.''

Ford: That's right. Now, the second major value of psychic awareness is that it gives proof of the immense power and worth of prayer, meditation, and the sacraments. These things are not just dead rituals or

[63]

fascinating traditions. They produce definite results on the inner planes that can be seen psychically.

Leichtman: What will it take to get the churches to begin appreciating the value of intuitive skills?

Ford: Well, it will take a great deal of time. Old ideas and beliefs change very slowly. I would hope that intelligent and mystical people everywhere would become a bit more courageous in talking about these things, explaining them to others, inviting those who do understand them to share their knowledge, and perhaps gather together a group of interested members of the congregation for a study group. There is a large body of occult literature available now about the inner side of church worship. Some of the books by Geoffrey Hodson and Bishop Leadbeater, for instance [*The Inner Side of Church Worship* and *Clairvoyant Investigations of Christian Origins and Ceremonials* by Hodson and *The Science of the Sacraments* and *The Hidden Side of Things* by Leadbeater], are writings that ought to be studied more widely. They describe the inner side of healing and what occurs when the sacraments are performed. These are books written by very competent and skilled clairvoyants who observed that when the sacraments are performed, angels literally are summoned and the Host bursts with light—a light that spreads over the whole congregation. The auras of everyone within the confines of the church and even outside the building are infused with new light.

If people could just appreciate what is really happening in their religious activities, they would be able to cooperate a bit more with the forces they invoke. Studying the works of competent, authoritative people, either by reading their books or by inviting them to give talks, can help us appreciate more the hidden side of life. There are a variety of excellent sources to draw upon.

Leichtman: You mentioned—

Ford: Excuse me. I'd like to give you another example. Clairvoyants have studied individuals while they were meditating or praying and have reported that friends from spirit—loved ones who have passed on, spirit guides, and angels—will draw near the earth plane during those times. This is especially true when the prayer or meditation is done within a group context. A group of people who gather for prayer invoke these things by their own love and intention.

Leichtman: You mentioned that if people could understand these spiritual influences, they would be better able to cooperate with the forces invoked in these ceremonies. What is the nature and benefit of this cooperation?

Ford: The benefit would be obvious. As you are able to believe in and comprehend the hidden nature of God, you can then invoke it to help you be a better person, to go through your daily activities with greater faith and conviction that there really is a benevolent intelligence that looks after you. Not just other people, but *you.* There is a benevolent intelligence that can inspire you to act with greater effectiveness and efficiency. There is a hidden, inner resource of power that gives you the courage to do the things you have to do and the strength to sustain you, heal you, and carry you beyond where you are now.

What I'm talking about is this—the higher psychic powers can be used to perceive the threshold of the kingdom of heaven—and beyond. Until the average person can comprehend that heaven is within us and around us, and that we are meant to interact with it, he cannot fully partake of its treasures of power, guidance, and love. So, by cooperation I mean a little extra faith here and a little extra courage there, study, and experimentation, leading ultimately to comprehension of the nature of these facts and forces. The higher type of psychic ability, then, helps us appreciate the power of a divinity that is ordinarily considered to be intangible and invisible.

Leichtman: You have been talking about lay people in the church. Would there be a benefit to a minister or priest to have intuitive capacities?

Ford: The value of the higher psychic powers in the clergy would be tremendous. Whether this perception is clairsentience, an inner knowing, or overt clairvoyance makes no difference. It adds to the pastor's intelligence and enriches his thinking and understanding about God and man. It adds an awareness of new possibilities and new ideas. This in turn strengthens faith. If you suddenly see something that you have always believed in, but have never before experienced, then obviously your faith is enormously strengthened.

Now, in all major religions, especially Christianity, the need for faith in invisible and intangible forces and intelligences is vital. The magnetic power of faith builds the bridge between heaven and earth, creating a magnetic channel through which the treasures of the kingdom of heaven can pass to earth. So, if the higher types of psychic awareness can increase faith, they ought to be respected and cultivated by the church.

Leichtman: Are you suggesting that the real work of a clergyman is to be a channel from heaven to earth?

Ford: Oh, absolutely. It's almost disgusting that some ministers and priests get caught up in being what amounts to a historian of biblical stories and dogma, an administrator of the church complex, a fund raiser, and an all-around spiritual dilettante. I very much appreciate that most ministers and priests have enormous responsibilities that are sometimes social, sometimes administrative, and sometimes supervisory. The church couldn't exist if these functions were ignored, but when a pastor works as a minister or priest to his flock, then he absolutely *must* transcend his own personality and be an agent of God. To do that, he must have greater faith and greater knowledge, and greater contact with the divine forces than almost anyone in the congregation. Perhaps the single most important quality he needs for that priestly function is the quality of love—the love of God, a reverence for God's ways, and a faith in God's works. In other words, he needs to be what I earlier called a mystic, loving all of life. With that love, he can be a better agent of God's illuminating light, grace, and power.

Leichtman: Very good. I've got a question of a slightly different nature, if you don't mind. Would there be a danger that a congregation might enshrine a person with higher psychic powers as some sort of saint or prophet?

Ford: I'll tell you a little secret here—to some extent, that is necessary. Worship of the personality is quite undesirable, because that focusses the attention on earthly things and detracts from the qualities and possibilities which are revealed by psychic and intuitive awareness. But when it come to martyrs, saints, apostles, Jesus, or any other prominent spiritual person of any religion, your reverence for them, their life, and their works magnetically attracts to you the force they represent. Devotion to Jesus or one of the saints magnetically puts you in contact with at least the fringes of their consciousness. Therefore, enshrining such people does have value, because it builds a bridge to something greater.

Now then, if you're dealing with someone with just a touch of clairvoyance—he sees some spirits going here and there and maybe a few auras—then obviously the veneration we've just been talking about would be inappropriate. Such a person can be helpful, but his talent must be kept in perspective. Unfortunately, there's a tendency for such people to think they are very special. Indirectly or directly they can stimulate a loyal following of devotees, at the expense of reverence for God. In essence, they form a mini-cult. That type of behavior is inimical to proper religious worship.

What is needed is more people who will dedicate their expression of extended awareness to being helpful in the world and to studying the spiritual implications of what they see. Sadly, there aren't too many psychics who are eager to do that. They may claim that they are, but then they don't behave that way. They have succumbed to the glamour of the psychic experience.

Each person needs to approach this subject with an awareness that there are a lot of things in the psychic realms which may be highly fascinating and absorbing, but they don't necessarily have value to him. Just as there are many things in the physical plane which are fun, exciting, glamorous, and beautiful, but don't particularly make you a better person, it's even more important to recognize this factor when dealing with the so-called psychic worlds. In the spiritual life, as well as in psychic endeavors, we are dependent upon the integrity, dedication, intelligence, and maturity of each aspirant. Nothing can replace these qualities.

I fear, Doctor, that I have broken my intention not to pontificate. [*Laughter.*]

Leichtman: Well, it's all for a good cause. What, if any, are the dangers of bringing psychic elements into a church setting? The fundamentalists always bring up the passage from Deuteronomy where the Jews are told that speaking with spirits and fortune telling are abominations unto the Lord. What is the proper perspective on that and what safeguards must be used?

Ford: Lots of things are abominations and ought to be avoided. At the top of my list would be bigotry, ignorance, malice, condemnation, and superstition. Those are far greater abominations than the lower forms of psychic silliness, which is what that passage in Deuteronomy warns against. One needs to keep this in perspective. I would suggest that readers take an hour or so and read as much of Deuteronomy as they can get through. [*Slyly*] Deuteronomy talks about what to do with a slave when you capture him, how to manage your concubines, and when it is proper to commit incest and murder. It is not fair to take what was once good advice, thousands of years ago, to a primitive, superstitious people and try to apply it in our own time.

Any time we are exploring new contacts, whether it's talking to a spirit, a psychic, a salesperson, a lawyer, a physician, or even a new minister, it is intelligent and spiritual to be somewhat cautious and thoughtful, until we have determined the nature of that person and his value to us. I'm not suggesting that everyone be paranoid or stubbornly cynical about these things, but it's human and intelligent to be careful. At the same time, however, it would be utterly silly to think that we are *forbidden* to talk to new people, to seek out a new minister or lawyer, or to consult a psychic or medium. Total censorship in these areas is not a spiritual idea at all. Let's face it—it's bigotry!

Yes, there are lots of rotten spooks, as well as silly ministers and arrogant health professionals and malicious people in all walks of life. In my book, they're *all* abominations. We should avoid them, but we should not avoid them blindly. We should see them for what they are and then make a discriminating choice based on our discernment.

God, after all, is a supernatural being. So is our own soul. Becoming psychic, which includes mediumship and clairvoyance, is one of the obvious ways to learn about and interact with a supernatural being. Ouija boards and gypsy fortune telling cards are not necessary, perhaps even harmful, but the higher forms of psychic perception are useful.

Leichtman: So it is safe to say that since God is not an abomination unto Himself, any means we successfully use to discern God cannot be an abomination.

Ford: Absolutely.

Leichtman: Is it all right to change subjects? We have talked a great deal about spirit guides—friends in the spirit who come to help us during our lifetime. What is the proper way of relating to these spirit entities?

Ford: Well, some people think of their spirit friends as some kind of free slaves. This is an abuse, because a spirit guide comes to you as a friend who wishes to share a life experience with you. Even though he is on a finer plane, he wishes to work with you on some particular aspect of your career—in and out of many physical lifetimes. For example, the two of you may have a mutual agreement to help one another in specific ways—with one working in the spirit and the other in the physical world. The roles may shift back and forth, but the friendship and the work continues on for many, many lifetimes.

That's the ideal, but it doesn't always print out that way. Another problem in these relationships, sometimes promoted by the Spiritualists, is the attitude that the physical person must surrender to the ''awesome wisdom and power'' of their spirit guides. [*Laughter.*] Spooks are not demi-gods. The proper way to relate to them is to realize that the essence of the relationship is *friendship*. Not worship or lordship.

Leichtman: Do you think some people have gone so far as to put their spirit guides *above God*?

Ford: That's abundantly obvious. Instead of rising up to God, many people find it easier to ''bring God'' down to their own level. As you know, many people also put their *own will* above God quite frequently. None of this is unusual—it's shameful, but not unusual.

Leichtman: Some people claim that Jesus could only do what He did because He had some unusually powerful spirit guides.

Ford: Or some help from a flying saucer! I've heard all these things, too. Of course, they're ridiculous. To put it very simply, Jesus was a person who so intimately knew the Father and the workings of the universe that He could perform seeming miracles. Now, when you say the word ''miracle,'' most people think of something like a fairy godmother touching you with a wand and turning you into a pumpkin. The miracles of a Master are not outside of science. They appear miraculous only because science is still outside of reality—science is just in the baby stage as yet. In other words, it doesn't understand all the workings of the universe.

I've often thought that it would be interesting if a Master were to spend a lifetime as a physicist, because not only would He be able to walk across the Sea of Galilee, but He would also be able to tell the rest of us how to do it.

As you know, Jesus is not the only Master. He is one of the great ones—and He's certainly the one most people know about—but He's not the only one.

Leichtman: How do the comments you've been making this afternoon apply to other religions?

Ford: The reason why I've been talking so much about putting psychic phenomena back into Christianity, and not other religions, is because most of my work in life was oriented toward formal Christianity. And, many of the other religions already have an awareness of the usefulness of the psychic experience within the church. We could indeed talk at great length about what other religions are doing with psychic phenomena, but I wanted to talk about what Christianity is *not* doing. It is making no attempt to use any of the mystical experience.

In my life, I tried to get this mystical experience

back into the church, where it belongs. I came to the conclusion that this was necessary, incidentally, by looking at what other religions were doing in this respect. I had the gift of mediumship, but I began to realize that there was no way I could use this gift in the ordinary practice of my Christian ministry.

Leichtman: I was going to ask you about your early training to be a minister. I made the comment laughingly before we started that you were not a ''five-dollar phony''; you were real.

Ford: I went through a seminary, yes. I was mediumistic before I started at the seminary. I worked very hard at becoming ordained. In my youth, I hoped I could make great inroads in the church and restore all this material. Very quickly I found I could not do so.

Leichtman: How about your early training as a medium?

Ford: Fletcher trained me more than anyone else. I'm sure David would say that Rosie trained him more than anyone else. Edgar Cayce would say that his friends trained him. This seems to be the way it works.

There are some other factors which influence the growth of a medium a great deal, too. The ways in which other people react to him are quite important. Edgar Cayce's life, for example, was such that his abilities could develop without friction. I was luckier than David in my selection of family, in that it was easier for me to enjoy my psychic gifts. Of course, I was very circumspect about my psychic abilities when I was young.

Getting through childhood can be very difficult for a person destined to be a medium. As a child, he may be very shy, easily frightened and frustrated, and a bit

[73]

nervous and sensitive. His interests and behavior may seem unusual at times. As a result, his family may misunderstand what's going on with him and get very upset. If the reaction of the family is improper, the child can easily develop some emotional problems.

In my case, I had a great deal of trouble as an adult relating to orthodox religion, and this was part of the reason why my alcoholism became very bad. I became very disappointed in my efforts to work in traditional Christianity—it didn't seem as though I was accomplishing anything. Faced with this disappointment and some other personal problems, alcoholism seemed to be my way out. I don't condone what I did. It did not make me a better medium. I lived through it— let's put it that way—but it's not recommended. I tried to describe these problems in some detail in *Nothing So Strange*.

Leichtman: Speaking of that, I recently heard someone accuse you, Arthur, of needing to have a lot to drink before you could function well as a medium. I didn't think that criticism was valid, but I do know some mediums and psychics feel they need to have a lot to drink or need to smoke pot before they can function adequately.

Ford: I did have a problem with drinking, yes, but it was not because it made me psychic. I don't recall ever telling anybody that I had to have a drink to make me psychic. Neither alcohol nor dope will make you psychic anyway.

Leichtman: None of them will make you psychic?

Ford: No. Sometimes, of course, when one is tense, having a drink or two before a reading will relax the psychic enough to carry on.

[74]

Leichtman: So, a cocktail or two doesn't really poison the psychic mechanism?

Ford: Oh, no. But, as I found out, getting carried away with it can distort a lot of things.

Leichtman: Is there any value in "sitting for development," as many people do in order to activate their mediumship?

Ford: Without belaboring a point that's already been made in these interviews, if the person that is conducting these sittings is not himself a medium, such training is not going to do any good whatsoever. Many of these groups get together and begin to feed their own hysteria—this is essentially what it is. They begin to get visions and voices, but they aren't real. They are hysterical visions and voices, not mediumship. It's unfortunate that this kind of thing even goes on.

I am glad, however, to see some more intelligent people involving themselves in psychic research than before. It helps expose the hysteria. In the past, many people were attracted to these groups because they gave them a convenient cover for their mental and emotional problems. They could meet once a week with a group of people who were just as immature and as hysterical as they were. The meetings gave them a way to vent their troubles and feed each other's problems. It was really more of a nonprofessional psychodrama than training for mediumship.

Leichtman: Yes. Let me ask this: I understand that you fully embrace the doctrine of reincarnation now. Was this part of your thinking or teaching when you were in the physical?

Ford: I had an understanding of it. I think most

psychics somehow sense that reincarnation is real. Fletcher and I never discussed it much, but remember, the format and context of our work did not lend itself to comments on reincarnation. We were, in a way, limited by our own ideas and by the people who came to us.

I did some reincarnation readings, but bear in mind that my work was not recorded as much as Edgar Cayce's. It was the work of Cayce and Joan Grant, I believe, that gave the impetus to the curiosity people now have in reincarnation. My work was in a different line.

If any three people in this room were to do readings on the same person or subject, independently, and then later compare notes, you would find that each psychic had gotten into different departments of that person or subject. You might all be right, but the readings would each be different. What any psychic reports is influenced by his point of view, what he's interested in, and what he's capable of receiving.

For instance, you could do a rather specific medical reading, because you know the names of all the parts you're looking at and their functions. If David did the same kind of reading, he could only guess and stammer and stutter—and then make a drawing of it. But you would be able to name the problem specifically.

Leichtman: To return to the subject of reincarnation, there are some mediums who state flatly that reincarnation is not a fact, because that's what their spirit guides say.

Ford: I'm going to quote one of your sayings, Doctor: just because somebody has passed over to the other side does *not* make him an expert! I tried to say this earlier: mediums should be very careful to evaluate the statements made by any spirit. The fact of the matter is that there aren't very many spirit guides coming through mediums who are Akashic readers. So, many spirit guides may not know much about reincarnation. Fletcher, for example, is not an Akashic reader. We did a little bit of this kind of reading, but we had to ask for help.

Leichtman: Well, that's all the questions I have. Arthur, are there people on the other side who wish to pass on a few words to people here? Would you be willing to help them come through?

Ford: Oh, yes—that would be a great pleasure. I was the David end of it, and now I get to be the Fletcher end of it. I enjoy it tremendously; I would be happy to do so.

[*The interview concluded with personal messages from deceased friends and relatives of the physical people present.*]

GLOSSARY

AKASHIC RECORDS: The cosmic record of events. On an individual basis, the Akashic is similar to the "memory" of the soul and therefore includes a record of all experiences of that soul, both in and out of incarnation.

ANGEL: An entity belonging to the angelic or devic kingdom. Angels are not discarnate humans and have never been humans—they are part of a separate kingdom of life, and have their own function and evolution. Still, their work and interests do bring them in touch with humans quite frequently—although humans are often unaware of this contact, as angels are invisible to ordinary sight. The angelic kingdom includes nature spirits, angels, and archangels. In *The Brotherhood of Angels and of Men*, Geoffrey Hodson says there are seven types of angels that commonly associate with man: angels of power, healing angels, angels of the home, building angels, angels of nature, angels of music, and angels of beauty and art. The word "angel" means "messenger."

ASTROLOGY: The science of the interplay of cosmic energies. Astronomy is the science of the interrelationship of physical bodies and energies in the universe; astrology is the science of the interrelationship of *all* bodies and forces in the cosmos—astral, mental, and even more rarefied ones, as well as physical.

AURA: The light observed by clairvoyants around all life forms. It emanates from the surface and interior of the etheric, astral, and mental bodies. Clairvoyant observation of the aura can give an indication of the quality of health or consciousness.

AVATAR: An entity who brings new elements or forces of heaven to earth, revealing their significance and how they can be attained. An avatar can be physical or nonphysical. The Buddha and the Christ were religious avatars, revealing the nature of wisdom and love. The work of an avatar is one of the highest forms of creativity.

BLACK MAGIC: The destructive manipulation of physical and emotional energies for selfish gain. It is the direct opposite of occultism, whose goal is to advance the life of the spirit.

CLAIRAUDIENCE: The capacity to hear nonphysical sounds, including voices, music, and mental impressions.

CLAIRSENTIENCE: The capacity to perceive or feel nonphysical impressions of ideas, emotions, spiritual qualities, and tangible events. It differs from clairaudience and clairvoyance in that clairsentient perceptions do not involve visual or verbal sensations.

CLAIRVOYANCE: The capacity to see or know beyond the limits of the physical senses. There are many degrees of clairvoyance, allowing the clairvoyant to comprehend forces, beings, and objects of the inner worlds normally invisible to the average person.

CLAIRVOYANT: Someone who has the faculty of clairvoyance. There are many levels of competence and many varieties of specialty among clairvoyants.

DISCARNATE: A human being without a physical body, living on the inner planes. Discarnates are also known as spirit entities or ''spooks.'' This is the state of human life in between physical lives.

ECTOPLASM: The etheric substance sometimes extruded by physical mediums while in trance. It resembles a luminous vapor, and can be used to move objects or provide a temporary vehicle for use by a discarnate.

ELEMENTAL: A primitive life form on the astral or etheric planes. Generally, the word refers to nature sprites.

ELVES: A type of nature sprite or elemental, typically associated with wooded areas. Elves are usually invisible, but can be seen clairvoyantly.

FORTUNE TELLER: A low-grade and silly type of psychic, who preys on the weaknesses and superstitions of his or her clients, rather than helping them understand more about their life and noble potential.

FOURTH DIMENSION: A realm of existence in which there can be four different planes of movement from a single point, each of those planes being separated by ninety degrees. The movement of a fourth-dimensional solid through the physical plane would be recognized as a change in the apparent three-dimensional shape of that object, as in the growth of a tree. We act in fourth-dimensional ways every day—by associating relevant memories to current experience, by speculating about our future, and by perceiving the underlying motives and attitudes of other people.

HEAVEN: The state of consciousness of the soul. Heaven is not a place populated by those who have died; it is accessible to incarnate and discarnate humans alike. It is a state of mind. In heaven are located the archetypal patterns of all Creation, as well as the ideal qualities of human expression. Heaven, therefore, is the source of all expression of genius and saintliness.

HOST: The bread of the Eucharist.

HYPNOSIS: A psychological technique for communicating more directly (and sometimes more forcefully) with the subconscious of an individual. It is an artificial technique which does not make contact with the inner being or soul of the individual, and is therefore limited in its usefulness.

I CHING: The Chinese Book of Changes. In popular use, it is a system of divination that uses pictograms and associated commentaries that are selected by the ''random'' fall of coins or sticks. Its purpose is to indicate the significance of any given event or condition, rather than reveal the future.

INNER PLANES: A term used to refer to any one of several inner worlds or levels of existence, all of which interpenetrate the dense physical plane. Each physical human being exists on these inner planes as well as on the physical level, by dint of having bodies composed of matter drawn from them. Most human beings do not consciously use these inner bodies, however, which either operate subconsciously or are partially inactive—until activated by personal growth and the development of intuitive awareness.

KARMA: A Sanskrit word meaning ''reactiveness.'' Every one of our actions, thoughts, and emotions produces a reaction of like quality, sooner or later. Good deeds and thoughts produce beneficent reactions; cruel or selfish deeds and thoughts produce restrictive reactions. By dealing with these karmic effects, we gradually learn the lessons of maturity.

MASTER: A term used by esoteric students to refer to an individual who has reached complete competence and perfection as a human. The epitome of genius.

MEDITATION: An act of mental rapport in which the ideals, purposes, and intents of the higher self are discerned, interpreted, and applied by the personality. To be meaningful, meditation must be a very active state in which creative ideas, new realizations, and inspirations are pursued with vigor.

MEDIUM: A person who practices mediumship by conscious choice.

MEDIUMSHIP: The phenomenon of a nonphysical intelligence, usually a discarnate human, assuming some degree of control of a physical body in order to communicate something useful and meaningful. Mediumship is usually used for the transmission of information and inspired guidance, but can also be used to transmit varieties of healing energies. There are varying degrees of trance associated with mediumship and differing qualities of information communicated, depending on the quality of the medium and the quality of the spirit using the process. Mediumship is distinguished from the phenomenon of possession in that it occurs only with the deliberate cooperation of the medium and produces a constructive result.

MYSTIC: One who seeks spiritual growth through mysticism.

MYSTICISM: The process of loving, revering, and *finding* God and His entire Creation.

OCCULT: The hidden secrets of nature. The study of the occult deals not just with the esoteric aspects of man's being, but also the entire universe. It includes the study of the function, operation, purpose, origin, and destiny of nature and man. The word ''occult'' literally means ''that which is hidden.''

ORACLE: A divine announcement or prophecy. The place where such a message is received, or the medium or psychic through which it comes, can also be called an oracle.

OUIJA BOARD: A silly device composed of a board on which the letters of the alphabet are printed and a planchette which is used to trace out messages, one letter at a time. Although most people using a Ouija board believe they are receiving messages from spirits, they are usually only in contact with the mischievous and deceptive portions of their subconscious. The Ouija Board is sold as a parlor game but can be very damaging to a person's psychological balance; it should never be used, even for entertainment.

PALMISTRY: A study of the symbolic significances of the lines of the hand. Palmistry is a tool of divination uniquely suited for investigating individual patterns of destiny.

PATH, THE: Personal commitment and dedication to spiritual aspiration and service. Occultly, the Path is the spiritual thread or connection that gradually forms between the soul and the personality during the evolution of human consciousness.

PERSONALITY: That part of a human being that is used for manifestation in the earth plane. It is composed of a mind, a set of emotions, and a physical body, each containing conscious and subconscious functions. It is the child of the soul and its experiences on earth.

POSSESSION: A condition in which a human personality is controlled and used by an entity other than the soul that created it, against the soul's will. It is a violation of cosmic law.

PRECOGNITION: The ability to foresee a future event before it happens.

PROPHET: One who speaks with divine inspiration. The words of a prophet may include predictions about the future, but they are not limited to that one function. More properly, a prophet reveals divine guidance for the benefit of mankind.

PSYCHIC: A person who is able to perceive events and information without the use of the physical senses. The word is also used to refer to any event associated with the phenomena of parapsychology.

READING: The act of relaying psychic or mediumistic information to a client. A psychic reading could also be called a psychic report or psychic consultation.

REINCARNATION: The concept that all inner beings evolve through a successive and progressive series of different physical personalities. The inner being finds it convenient and most practical to use a sequence of different personalities, covering millions of years, to fulfill its ultimate purpose. Reincarnation should not be mistaken for ''transmigration,'' a spurious doctrine that suggests that human entities can return in future lives as different kinds of animals. Reincarnation refers only to the use by the inner being of successive human personalities to achieve mastery.

SEANCE: The event of a discarnate spirit entity speaking through a medium, in order to communicate with physical people.

SIBYL: A woman serving as an oracle.

SITTING: A seance.

SOUL: The individualized principle of consciousness and creativity within the human being. It is the soul that evolves and acts; it is the soul that creates the potential of the personality, vivifies it, and guides it through certain life experiences designed to increase competence in living. The soul is a pure expression of love, wisdom, and courage; its identity is not damaged by changes or tumults in the life of the personality—even death or rebirth.

SPIRIT: In this book, a term used primarily to describe the portion of the human being that survives death. It is this ''spirit'' that a medium contacts. In this sense, a spirit would be as individualistic as his or her personality was during physical life, retaining both good and bad characteristics. The word is also used to refer to the highest immortal, divine essence within the human being.

SPIRIT CONTROL: A special type of discarnate human who works with a medium. The function of the spirit control is to guard the ''doorway'' to the medium's mind, to act as master of ceremonies for other spirits who might appear through the medium, and to care for the condition of the medium's body before and during the medium's trance period.

SPIRIT GUIDE: A discarnate human who, out of friendship, helps a physical human being during his or her lifetime.

SPIRITUALISM: A religious movement that incorporates mediumship as a central feature of its worship service and investigation of spiritual values.

SPOOK: An affectionate term for a discarnate.

SUBCONSCIOUS: The part of the personality that is not being consciously used at any given moment. The subconscious is always active and greatly influences our conscious moods, thoughts, acts, and attitudes. It is psychically in tune with other portions of the inner planes—even if we are not consciously psychic at all.

TRANCE: A state in which ordinary consciousness is quieted so that another element of consciousness can use the physical voicebox and body. In a hypnotic or drug-induced trance, the subconscious assumes control of the body. In a mediumistic trance, another entity takes over. A trance state often seems to resemble sleeping, but is actually much different: the physical body remains responsive and can be used actively.

VAMPIRE: One who saps or steals energy from another individual telepathically or psychically.

VIBRATION: The movement of any energy particle, whether physical, astral, or mental in origin. The word is popularly used to refer to emanations of astral energy that are perceived by psychic sensitivity.

FROM HEAVEN TO EARTH

The complete series of 12 interviews is available by subscription for $27 (for overseas delivery, $30). Each interview is published as a paperback book such as this one.

The spirits interviewed are Edgar Cayce, William Shakespeare, Cheiro, Carl Jung and Sigmund Freud, C.W. Leadbeater, Sir Oliver Lodge, Thomas Jefferson, Arthur Ford, H.P. Blavatsky, Nikola Tesla, Eileen Garrett, and Stewart White. All 12 books are now in print.

Orders can be placed by sending a check for the proper amount to Ariel Press, 2557 Wickliffe Road, Columbus, Ohio 43221-1899. Please make checks payable, in U.S. funds, to Ariel Press, or charge to MasterCard, VISA, or American Express. Ohio residents should add 5½% sales tax.

Individual copies of the interviews are also available, at $3 plus $1 postage each, when ordered from the publisher. When 10 or more copies of a *single* title are ordered, the cost is $2 per book plus the actual cost of shipping.

These books may also be purchased through your favorite bookstore.

THE PRIESTS OF GOD

Due to the popularity of the first series of 12 books in *From Heaven to Earth*, a second series of 12 interviews is also being conducted by Dr. Robert R. Leichtman and is available by subscription.

The spirits interviewed in this second series are all individuals who demonstrated a remarkable capacity to act with genius, leadership, and inspiration in their respective fields. The 12 spirits are Albert Schweitzer, Rembrandt, Sir Winston Churchill, Paramahansa Yogananda, Mark Twain, Albert Einstein, Benjamin Franklin, Andrew Carnegie, Richard Wagner, Luther Burbank, and Abraham Lincoln. The final book will be an interview with a number of spirits, titled *The Destiny of America*. A new book is published every three months. The series will be completely in print by October 1983.

The cost of subscribing to all 12 books is $27, postpaid. Orders can be placed by sending a check for the proper amount to Ariel Press, 2557 Wickliffe Road, Columbus, Ohio 43221-1899. Make checks payable to Ariel Press. Foreign checks should be payable in U.S. funds. Orders can also be charged to MasterCard, VISA, or American Express. In Ohio, please add 5 ½ % sales tax.

Individual copies of the interviews are available at $3 plus $1 postage each. If 10 or more copies of *a single title* are ordered at one time, the price is $2 a book plus the actual costs of shipping.